Endorsements

*****

"Tina Chadda's heartfelt evocation of the power of attention, presence and kindness offers a compelling guide for moving beyond just the remission of symptoms and syndromes into a landscape where fuller, vibrant living is well within reach."
~Zindel V. Segal, Ph.D., C.Psych.
Distinguished Professor of Psychology
in Mood Disorders
Department of Psychology
University of Toronto - Scarborough

*****

"I highly recommend "The Heart that Heals Itself: Discovering Emotional Riches through Meditations & Reflections" by renowned psychiatrist Tina Chadda. In her book Dr. Chadda focuses on love, connection, spirituality, mindfulness and self-healing. Her book is a journey through looking inward and achieving peace of mind and love through self-reflection and meditation. The knowledge and inspiration

found in this book is useful to practitioners of healing and to those seeking to transform their heart. I felt uplifted and inspired and I am sure you will too."
~Dr. Mel Borins, Author, Public Speaker and Family Physician

*****

"Dr. Tina Chadda's "heart", in which body and mind combine, is the fulcrum where feelings and intellect meet. At this juncture we can explore balance and peace, and this can ultimately lead to the evolution of a more clearly delineated self."
~Dr. Cinda Dyer, MD, FRCPC, Psychiatrist, Psychoanalyst

*****

"This book is based on the author's personal and professional understanding of suffering as an inevitable, and hence, vital aspect of the human condition. It is a wise and valuable antidote for the pathologies created by rampant materialist consumerism and the notion that we are what we can buy/possess. Unlike most psychological "self help" books it is free of academic jargon. Its sincerity and simplicity of style enables the reader to gain a deeper understanding of the nature of

his/her suffering and cope with it in a creative and transforming way. Drawing from various non-western spiritual traditions, the author suggests a range of holistic therapeutic strategies which can be easily incorporated into daily practice. Written from the heart, this book educates and inspires the 'broken' heart by awakening it to the healing power of love and compassion which is at the core of our humanity – and all spiritual traditions."
~Durre S. Ahmed, Ed.D. Consultant Psychologist, Chairperson and Senior Research Fellow Center for the Study of Gender and Culture Lahore, Pakistan

*****

"The Heart that Heals Itself is an inspiring guide to the process growing out of adversity. Combining concepts of Vedanta with Dr. Tina Chadda's professional experience, it is a comprehensive, actionable book that is both spiritual and practical at the same time."
~Ran Zilca,
Author of Ride of Your Life, a Coast-to-Coast Guide to Finding Inner Peace

*****

"From the heart-centered mind of psychiatrist Dr. Tina Chadda, these words are designed to help you upgrade your well-being. The inspirational combination of meditation and mindfulness complements therapy and coaching, and empowers you to spend more time in a peaceful, contented state. I wholeheartedly recommend this book."
~Margaret Moore, MBA, a/k/a Coach Meg CEO, Wellcoaches Corporation Co-Founder/Co-Director, Institute of Coaching McLean Hospital, Harvard Medical School affiliate

*****

"The Heart That Heals Itself is a beautiful, profound and unique book that offers the pathway to open your heart to experience greater joy and a rich fullness of life."
~Peggy McColl, New York Times Best Selling Author

*****

"The Heart that Heals Itself is a must-read for anyone who is ready to enjoy a life filled

with love and serenity. Tina Chadda's meditations will help you find all the emotional riches you seek while creating more balance in your life."
~Jennifer Colford, International Best Selling Author: Managing Mothering

*****

"This insightful and wonderfully written book encourages the reader to reflect and look inside for self-discovery. Understanding how important it is to heal our heart and fill it with love allows us to let the hurt go and move on. Reading and meditating on each chapter lets the reader feel more relaxed and open to healing. I encourage any person who has been hurt to read this book and feel the freedom of opening their heart."
~Alena Chapman, Author of You Can't Escape From A Prison If You Don't Know You're In One

The Heart that Heals Itself

Discovering Emotional Riches through Meditations & Reflections

By

Tina Chadda, M.D.

The Heart that Heals Itself © 2015.
All rights reserved by Tina Chadda, MD.

W & B Publishers

For information:
W & B Publishers
Post Office Box 193
Colfax, NC 27235
www.a-argusbooks.com

ISBN: 978-0-692326305

Book Cover designed by Maria Marotta

Printed in the United States of America

Acknowledgments

I thank my family for their patience and support while I wrote this book.

My children - Priyanka, Armaan, Gaurav, and Aarav – you are my world. You are truly God's gifts to me. Every moment of each day is richer because of each of you. Through you I have discovered how wonderfully powerful and positive parent-child love can be.

I thank my husband, Anoop, for his support.

Gurbachan Singh Kindra, my late maternal grandfather, I am grateful to you for conversations in India. From you, I learned about Partition, politics, philosophy and religion. You taught me about the fierce tenacity of the human spirit and the quest for survival and betterment. I thank you for my love of spirituality, love of conversation, and curiosity of literature and poetry.

I thank my patients for revealing your internal landscapes to me, and for trusting me with the most intimate details of your lives. I learn from each of you and I have tremendous respect for the conversations we have with one another. Each therapy session I conduct reminds me that the human struggle and desire for love and healing is universal.

I thank the following people: Justin Spizman, my book architect and editor, Peggy McColl for general guidance, Michael Barbarulo for an introduction to the world of publishing, and Maria Marotta for design assistance.

Table of Contents

Foreword

Preface

Dear Reader

Section One: Love

- How to Get Love in Your Life
- How to Create More Love
- Noticing Love
- Why I Need to Love Myself
- Love as the Highest Emotion
- Love as Decision
- The Secret Language of Self-Love
- Ahimsa as Love
- Keeping the Doors of Love Open
- My Self-Esteem is Preserved in My Heart
- How to Increase Self-Worth
- Towards a Working Definition of Love
- Parent-Child Love
- Flow as Love
- A Special Poem about Love

Foreword

What do we mean when we say that love is blind? True love is the acceptance of who we are. It does not see our faults. Each time a woman, who was receiving chemotherapy, finished her chemotherapy session she would vomit all the way home, her husband would hand her a bag to throw up in. One day he handed her the bag, and when she opened it she found a dozen roses inside. To him she was still beautiful. His blindness, his love for her, resulted in her never being sick after therapy again.

True love is blind to our mistakes, faults, and moments of weakness, thus opening the door to healing. Love is the answer to every problem, and I mean that literally. Love benefits the giver and the receiver. As Emmett Fox once said, "If only you could love enough, you would be the happiest and most powerful person in the world." Loving others is a miracle-making attitude, a love-warrior way of being, which benefits the giver and receiver and self-love is where it all begins.

When Tina Chadda went to medical school she was influenced by the writings of a few doctors at the forefront of a pivotal time in modern day medicine. She devoured the words of people such as me, Deepak Chopra, and others – healers who came from an educational background of hard core science, and yet we proposed that mind, heart, and soul needed as much attention as the body. In my case, I trained as a surgeon, but I learned through the experience of working with patients, both before and after surgery, that healing is not just about cutting out the disease, so much as it is about dealing with what is wrong with - or missing in - the person's life. You cannot separate feelings and health. Mind, emotions, and body are parts of one unit. And suffering or recovering individuals need to find a way to heal and grow *within*. This can only happen in an internal environment of love. We need to treat the cause and not just the result.

I retired from surgery in the late 1980s and began to help people heal in a different way. My first book, *Love, Medicine and Miracles,* helped to change the way the medical profession thinks about patients, disease, and treatment. I formed support groups for cancer patients, lectured across the country, and wrote many books. Sharing my own explorations and experience, I helped to nudge open previously closed doors to the mind-body-spirit approach to medicine and healing in the western world. I shared what I and my patients found - that practices such as meditation and creative visualization are not adjunctive therapies so much as essential parts of the healing process and building blocks that may be used for the rest of a person's life.

I am so pleased to learn that my work became a backdrop for Tina's practice with her patients. Each one of us is a seed in the garden of life; each one of us produces our own unique leaves, flowers, and fruits. But the message we all teach is the same – it's a message of authentic growth, healing, and love.

Tina has spoken to me of her work as a psychiatrist and therapist. Just as a surgeon helps to eliminate acute symptoms caused by disease, she helps people to become free of problematic psychological symptoms. After dealing with acute symptoms such as depression or anxiety, the initial lack or cause of the problem still needs to be faced. Tina spoke of this process as moving from being stuck in the dark basement, to climbing up to ground level and into the light. But clear ground can leave people feeling empty or neutral, clinically referred to as symptom free, or in remission. The challenge is to replace the old problem-causing thoughts and beliefs with something that is healthy, loving, and promotes creativity and inner growth. I call it reparenting. Tina calls it heart-healing.

When you choose to love your life your body's internal chemistry is changed. Amazing things happen as your immune system strives to keep you healthy and your body's natural rhythm and balance return. Let your pains become labor pains which lead you to create and constantly rebirth a new life. Your loving attitude toward self will help others to survive too. Using the techniques that Tina shares - mindfulness and meditation - you will pay attention to your thoughts and experience the accompanying feelings. You will realize without a doubt that mind and heart do matter; that you can recreate your inner environment and abandon the wounds of your past and childhood.

To achieve this one needs to have a quiet mind, like that of a still pond. This symbol, found in many myths, allows you to see your true identity, your authentic self. When you are thinking and worrying the turbulence blocks your ability to see that beautiful, lovable self, just as the ugly duckling did not know he was a swan until he saw his reflection on a still pond.

Through my medical career and personal life, I came to appreciate the power of using a daily practice of meditation, appropriate prayer, or mantra. This gives people a path to their spirituality, a way to connect with their own divine nature and to change negative thoughts and beliefs into loving, positive knowledge of who they really are. True healing occurs on physical, emotional, *and* spiritual levels.

Tina's experience and wisdom can coach you and help you to create love for yourself and others. Join us on this path of heart-healing. Read on and let Tina's wisdom and guidance help you to heal your heart and your life. Carry the message of Tina's words, choose life and live the sermon of love.
~Dr. Bernie S. Siegel

Preface

Tina has, with her characteristic courage, leapt into the vast waters of Love. She has given us a book that is a compilation of thoughts, meditations, poems gleaned from her own life and the writings of others.

This book is an intimate journey with the author as she explores her relationships, her emotions and beliefs around the subject with the goal of being a resource that you may read through or pick up and open a page and read and absorb the message therein.

As a psychiatrist Tina has had plenty of exposure to human suffering and her writings can serve as a starting point from which we can move into a closer relationship with our own emotional landscape. The reflections can be an antidote for suffering giving the reader points of learning, a guided meditation time or a phrase which can serve as a consolation or a deepening of a moment in your emotional journey for the day. I found the work accessible, and a wonderful addition to the wealth of writings that deal with our preoccupations with this human need.

Dear reader, keep this book at hand be it by your bed or comfortable chair and allow the love, the wisdom and compassion of Dr. Tina Chadda to become a companion in your life. Share it with your family and friends so that you can create your own community of love.

Love is the apex of a multifaceted indescribable jewel comprising such elements as forgiveness, compassion, mindfulness, peace, joy to name a few. Tina wants the reader to appreciate their own wondrous beauty, simply and gently. Enjoy this work!

~Anne Hennessy, MB BCh BAO, BA, FRCPC
Ottawa, Canada

Introduction

Dear Reader,

This book is for you. Yes, just you! This collection of meditations and reflections was created as a mixture of knowledge and inspiration, support and strength, guidance and direction.

My fascination with the symbolism of the heart was precipitated by a series of events that made me understand our truest and deepest healing lies in the vast landscape of the heart. While I am a trained psychiatrist, I received these insights through my personal life, not my professional one. During an extremely tumultuous period, I began to pay close attention to the topic of what true healing really is and from where it originates.

Until several years ago, I didn't take the subject of "healing the heart" all that seriously. At that time my own life fell apart in so many serious ways. I'd lost everything in a house fire – on Valentine's Day. I'd narrowly escaped with my two youngest children. The other two were at school, and my husband was at work. My family and I were then without a permanent home for a long time, and just as we managed to recreate our home, my husband was diagnosed with cancer. Superimposed on all of this was a drawn-out legal battle over insurance issues related to the financial loss of our original home and then building its replacement.

From this this period of deep darkness I learned that life can change in a single heartbeat. It can change for the worse, or the better. One single, solitary heartbeat is all it takes for your life to go in an entirely different direction.

We all have challenges to overcome. From the outside your life's challenges may not necessarily seem tragic or look terrible. Only you can understand the full impact that your situation has on your heart.

The heart has memory. Any suffering you experience is simultaneously absorbed and revealed by all the layers of your heart. We each have experiences with the potential to shut the door to our hearts. For some, this door stays closed forever. Yet each of us has the capacity and resources within to coax this door open.

Healing your heart is the most important and valuable thing you can do in your life. Your capacity to enjoy the beauty of life, to love yourself, and to love others actually depends on it. Your expanded state of awareness is the gateway to your soul; learning to work with yourself and to experience real transformation happens first in your life and then in the world around you. The process of transformation itself is an act of self-love.

I encourage you to look within and get in touch with your heart – the core of your being or your essence. From this heart-centered vantage point, consider your stance towards life and your own healing. Healing means restoring, fixing, or bringing back to a state of health or soundness. If you're going to take the effort to repair a situation, why not transform it, ground it in character strengthening, and make it even better than it was before?

The majority of my medical career has been spent practicing as a psychiatrist helping patients manage mood and relationship issues, post-traumatic situations, and serious medical conditions using a variety of psychotherapeutic modalities. My areas of subspecialty are psychotherapy and psychosomatics (the mind-body interface), and I have trained in eating disorders and psycho-oncology. More recently, I have become interested in mindfulness and meditation, and I use these practices with my patients and myself. I am influenced by my Eastern heritage as well as by Western traditions.

Over decades of working with thousands of patients, I have been closely observing the differences between remission, well-being, and healing. I have come to understand that the difference between just coping and healthy functioning is similar to that between surviving and thriving. Moreover, I have seen that freedom from illness or suffering doesn't necessarily allow you to love the life you once had. True healing is a transformative process that picks up where successful medical treatment leaves off. You must actively pursue it. Because the fullness of our lives is experienced in the heart, the active pursuit of happiness and healing must be heart-focused.

Deep within us, at the authentic core of the heart, is where we hold the values that are dearest and truest to us. But here is where most people feel a lack, rather than an abundance, of emotional wealth, and we often experience a sense of imbalance. The search to overcome the "something is missing" phenomenon in our lives and hearts is our greatest challenge. This may be experienced in general daily unhappiness, stress, existential loneliness, inferiority complex, feeling broken in some way, or simply an overall poverty of emotional experience. How, then, can you heal such broad areas as these?

The answer lies in turning to the heart. Through mindful awareness, self-nourishment, and self-nurturance, our internalized values will grow into more enduring states of being. In other words, it is possible to solidify the simply passing states that we enjoy into lasting ones that we then term "character." These may be creativity, light-heartedness, patience, curiosity, forgiveness, or any number of other positive and loving traits that enrich and fulfill our lives when we seed and absorb them into our hearts.

The quest for a happy heart is a good, worthwhile journey. In fact, I believe it to be the ultimate journey. An open heart-mind, in combination with a curious brain-mind, gives you a formidable, more complete intelligence with which to face life's challenges and to recognize all that life offers.

From my heart to yours, I promise that you will find these words healing. These simple yet sophisticated reflections will work wonders in your life. I invite you to bravely step into your own heart and discover the abundance of riches that are waiting for you.

With Love,
Tina
Toronto, Canada

Section One: Love

"The consciousness of loving and being loved brings a warmth and a richness to life that nothing else can bring."

Oscar Wilde

Love is that elusive life-giving elixir that lubricates the machinations of our lives. It is a necessary condition of life and without it, we wither away, and even die. We hugely debate the definition of love and even misunderstand it.

We don't always recognize love per se, but we certainly recognize the presence or the absence of it. It can be a warming sensation, comforting and supportive in otherwise dark corners. It uplifts, inspires, and motivates courage and strength. It makes your heart beat faster and stronger and pushes you to

far greater achievements and accomplish-
ments than you ever thought possible.

Beyond the familiar romantic or erotic
aspects of love, there is love of community,
love of friends, love of children, love of
togetherness, love of solitude, love of
nature, love of books, love of food, love of
music, love of travel, love of beauty, love of
freedom, love of country, love of language,
love of art, love of health, love of
achievement, love of vitality, love of sport,
love of pets, love of knowledge, love of
design and fashion, love of summer, love of
sleep, love of the self. Then there is love as
virtue, love as compassion, love as
admiration, love as enthusiasm, love as nonviolence, love as the essence of a
relationship, love as devotion, love as
discipline, love as respect, love as kindness,
love as loyalty, love as empathy, love as
surrender, love as truth, love as creation,
love as the ultimate truth, love as Universe,
and love of love itself.

How to Get Love in Your Life

It's simple.

Forget about yourself. Give your undivided, heartfelt and sincere attention to the other person. Pay complete attention to the person in front of you. And expect nothing in return.

Have you ever watched a mother with her newborn baby?

She's completely forgotten about herself. She is providing her child with total love and isn't expecting anything in return. Ask her if she feels loved: she will tell you she is deliriously in love with her baby, and that she feels the love in return. This is because in the process of her giving love, she has received love from the infant who has not done anything active to elicit this response. The connection is undeniable. The vibrant exchange of love is unspoken and powerful.

Yes, relationships get more complicated as time goes on, but the principles hold true even as time clouds these special moments of beginnings.

How to Create More Love

This is what to do when you feel you need love. When nourished and given attention, love can expand.

Close your eyes and breathe slowly from and through your heart-center. Think of someone, living or passed, who loves you.

In order to allow for a full sensory experience, visualize this person before you in as much detail as possible. Allow yourself to feel the love emanating from this person and O-P-E-N your heart to the love that is coming to you.

Take it into your heart as you breathe. Focus on this feeling of love, and visualize it growing within you as you continue to breathe.

Noticing Love

Pay attention now. No matter how much you think you know about love, the smallest, most infinitesimal internal quaver is the most useful evidence you'll ever get. You may not know what it means right now, but what's important is simply to notice it. No one taught you what to do with these faint stirrings. You weren't taught to be aware of them, and you weren't taught to disregard them either. Do they really exist? You thought they weren't significant because they were occurring within you. What do you know? You know a lot; you know more than you think you know.

Keep noticing what you notice about love and meticulously work to open your eyes just a little wider. Notice something new each and every day.

Why I Need to Love Myself

Sometimes I am better at loving others than loving myself. I am noticing that if I do not love myself, either through self-neglect or not letting others love me, I create a state of imbalance within myself. It hurts my heart and thus hurts my life. Paying attention to the influx and out flux of love in my heart helps me to achieve a state of inner balance and well-being.

In being mindful about loving myself, I am working on cultivating my best self. It is from this resourceful state that I can offer the most to others and the world around me.

Love as the Highest Emotion

Love, in ordinary everyday life, is the highest emotion we are capable of experiencing. It is a truly heartfelt way of being with others and it begins with the emotional-self. It is about being present and connected to the world around us. It is expressed in a myriad of ways, always being characterized by warmth, gratitude, purity, and sweetness. When we are generous, kind, even-natured, forgiving, nurturing, protective, collaborative, and caring we are being loving to others and welcoming in the most powerful emotions we can experience.

Love as Decision

Love is a noun, a verb, and an experience;
it's a choice and a decision, and most
importantly and simply, a way of being. It's
really a decision about existing in a loving
way. This is a way of being that arises as we
drop all else, letting the lower emotions go
and focusing on this potent feeling. It means
overcoming our narcissism, transcending the
needs of the self to connect with that which
has meaning. This way of being with others
promotes harmony and peace.

The Secret Language of Self-Love

I am in this moment. I will not judge myself. I accept where I am while I continue to seek bliss. I will go at my own pace and not worry about the pace of those around me. I am fine as I am. I like myself as I am. I love myself as I am.

Ahimsa as Love

Ahimsa, the first of the Patanjali Yoga Sutra yamas, is often translated as "nonviolence." But the concept of ahimsa is more subtle and more beautiful than this. If you take into consideration that "yama" literally means death, it's easy to see that Patanjali intended us to see the concept of ahimsa as the death of violence, rather than nonviolent.

We are frequently violent with our words and thoughts. The thought-power that we exert when we think negatively, aggressively or not in a loving fashion is extremely strong. Practicing ahimsa means to constantly use our meta-cognition, or our self-awareness of thinking, to observe ourselves as we relate to both others and ourselves.

Women are frequently self-critical of themselves and their body image: should I have that second piece of cake, or shouldn't I? The inner dialogue of harsh scrutiny can escalate to a point of being considered violent. Eating disorders can be seen as a powerful example of violence towards the self in our culture. Addictions are perhaps another example.

Ahimsa means letting criticism, gossip, sarcasm, and self-loathing die off. Let positive thoughts and feelings enter, take root and flourish. Ahimsa originates from the heartfelt intention to act with clarity and love. Giving love with conditions is violence; unconditional love is ahimsa.

Try going through one entire day practicing ahimsa towards yourself. Through mindful awareness make every thought, feeling, and action as positive and loving as possible. It must be genuine or heartfelt. See how you feel at the end of the day in comparison to a usual day. My guess is love will be at the forefront of your emotions.

Keeping the Doors of Love Open

Sometimes the doors that let love into my heart are violently slammed shut by hurt. It could come in the form of a big hurt or even a small one.

The slamming part is easy, but the unjamming part is more of a challenge. As I recognize the need to simply pay attention to keeping these doors open, I am able to experience more love in my life. I do this by resolving the hurt through understanding, learning, and forgiveness. As I do this, I become more resilient and less hypersensitive. With constant practice, the doors don't close so often. Our goal should be to keep the doors of love wide open at all times.

My Self-Esteem is Preserved in My Heart

When I am stressed, my self-esteem begins to dissolve and melt away. However, I remind myself that it is preserved in my heart-mind and heart-soul. I seek out my precious self-esteem, and it is always there for me, and in doing so it remains intact and can inevitably grow.

How to Increase Self-Worth

I begin by focusing on something I believe to be worthy within me, such as a talent or virtue. Alternatively, I look for a quality in myself that I may undervalue, overlook, or even under-appreciate. I stay with this for a few moments and concentrate on it, deeply looking into and reflecting within my heart. I imagine this trait growing within my heart, and I begin to feel better.

In this way, I can grow my self-worth in my heart.

Towards a Working Definition of Love

There are so many definitions of love. A modern, practical working definition of love comes from the world of Positive Psychology. Barbara Fredrickson, an American psychologist, in her research on positivity, indicates that we can view love as the culmination of the nine following positive emotions: joy, gratitude, serenity, interest, hope, pride, amusement, inspiration and awe.

Love completes the list of ten positive emotions.

This framework is useful as it encompasses the wonderful range of positive feeling-states and because it is free from any sort of recipe or dosing regimens. Any or all of the positive emotions can go into the mix, in any quantity.

Parent-Child Love

"Dear Mum,

Thank you for always supporting me (like when you drive me to rowing) and doing all the things you do for us. Thanks for being the best Mum and Happy Birthday."

What a beautiful birthday message I received from my young daughter! I was overcome with joy, and it was nice to know that my daughter appreciated some of the things I do for her.

Children notice a lot, much more than their verbal capacity allows them to outwardly indicate. Most importantly, they notice your demeanor as you parent, and the tone and the underlying feeling and emotion behind how you, as a parent, perform these tasks for them.

Being a parent is hard work and involves serious transcending of the self. The process of transcending is the very essence of the love that you share with your child. Be proud of all the things you can do for your children, even the smallest of things. Congratulate yourself for your ever-growing capacity to love your child. Making lunches early in the morning, cuddling in the evening, and folding laundry together become intimate acts of love if you can transcend your resistances or desire to do more "worthwhile" or "grownup" things with your time.

Your mindful awareness of your child's subjective experience is a huge, invisible gift that you can give each day, and this has lasting value in your child's life. Don't make the mistake of discounting the importance of these activities simply because you may view them as mundane and repetitive. It's a bonus if your child notices your efforts, especially the seemingly insignificant ones, and reflects that love back to you.

Flow as Love

Mihaly Csikszenthmihalyi studied the phenomenon known as "flow" and brought it into the mainstream. He used this word to describe a state in which one acts effortlessly and is completely absorbed in the activity itself. In a state of flow, time seems to stand still and it is as if you become one with the activity itself. His writings emphasize that in a state of flow, the heart, mind, and will act seamlessly together, culminating in tremendously satisfying experiences. Much of the academic research on flow comes from studying Olympic athletes in their states of peak performance. Ordinary everyday activities like making love, reading an enjoyable book, playing the piano or cooking are flow states too. Flow is characterized by a sense of deep satisfaction and may or may not be accompanied by an even deeper sense of euphoria.

Flow as deep satisfaction can be seen and experienced as love and happiness.

A Special Poem about Love

The world's literary library is filled with poems about love. Here is an addition by my dear friend and colleague Dr. Vinod Bhardwaj. He wrote it following an intense debate over whether love is a privilege or a pleasure.

LOVE IS A PRIVILEGE

Once upon a time
Said a wise Sage
Living is an act
Life is a stage
Script is allegoric
Deceptive each phrase
An album of memories
Surprise on every page
The theme is often happy
And at times full of rage
It's essence is imbibed
In final words of sage
Loving someone is a pleasure
Being loved is a privilege.

My Rose Garden

The rose has signified beauty, passion,
grace, purity, success and the divine since
ancient times. As an unparalleled and
timeless expression of love, a single rose can
readily become a centerpiece in the human
heart. The unfurling of a rosebud, in and of
itself, is a multi-layered and endless
discourse in the unfolding of oneself in
relation to the self and to the other, as well
as an unfolding of the universe. No other
flower carries the tender and powerful
immediacy of love like a rose.

Here's my take on a favorite childhood
verse.

Roses are red,
Violets are blue.
Anoop - you and I - two rare flowers –
resulted in six,
A delightful, heady and divine mix.

Roses are red,
Violets are blue.
Priyanka, your name means beloved;
you came like an angel from above,
Purifying me with an unearthly surge of
parent-child love.

Roses are red,
Violets are blue.
Armaan, true to your name, you help to
fulfill my purpose and longing,
To make a family of my own where there is
a joy of belonging.

Roses are red,
Violets are blue.
Gaurav, blessed with boundless energy, you
are named for soul's pride.
Let your free spirit be gently guided as you
keep your unique stride.

Roses are red,
Violets are blue.
Aarav – an unexpected rose dropped from
God's hand into mine – you really are peace,
With you, my heartfelt desire for a family I
could finally release.

Roses are red,
Violets are blue.
My sweet children, listen now: be like a
flower,
Forever in touch with your personal power.

Roses are red,
Violets are blue.
Your show is what the world will see,

Most beautiful when the essence of you is
all it can possibly be.

Roses are red,
Violets are blue.
Trying to nurture you with my love is my
greatest pleasure,
To watch each of you blossom, is a
fulfillment of endless measure.

Love

Love is truly the culmination of our heart and soul. It transcends time and space and nudges us to surpass the best of what we have to offer. But more than anything, love connects people to one another. It is the unseen but present and powerful relationship between a husband and wife, mother and daughter, dog and his owner, brother and his sister, father and son. It is an emotion that takes time to develop, but once formed, is forged in steel and amazingly sturdy, reliable and difficult to break. Love moves people to action and creates unparalleled warmth and glow that can be seen from miles away. Love is so much more than we can collectively describe or even understand. But it all starts with a desire to build a meaningful connection with someone else.

Section Two: Connection

"We cannot live only for ourselves. A thousand fibers connect us with our fellow men; and among those fibers, as sympathetic threads, our action run as causes, and they come back to us as effects."

Herman Melville

The desire to feel connected runs deep inside each of us. It could be to people, to nature, to animals, to an idea, or even to a coveted possession. Regardless, we all want to awake each and every day and feel the warmth that connection injects into our hearts and souls. No one wants to live life in a disconnected or isolated manner. To be connected is to be alive.

Nothing connects us more than our heart. It is the center of our body and pumps blood carrying vital nutrients and oxygen throughout the body. If blood is our fuel, then the heart is the engine that facilitates its delivery. Without the heart, there could be no uniformity and no connectivity amongst the rest of our body. Our heart connects us inwardly by moving rich blood cells throughout our body and outwardly through those moments when it beats just a little faster as we begin to build a strong connection with another person.

Connection is the product of a desire to relate, to communicate, and to exist in the moment. When connection grows strong, love begins to shine through. As much as love is many things to many people, in its simplest form, it is an unbreakable and unwavering connection between two people.

A Heart-Connection with Yourself

Place your right hand over your chest, slightly to the left of the middle. Mentally bring your attention there. You may feel a sense of warmth. Feel the beating of your heart. Mindfully breathe your energy in and out of your heart-center. Do this for several minutes. Anchor your breath and attention to your heart-center. Acknowledge yourself. Be calm. Be centered.

Queen and Subject

In my heart I can exist as queen and subject.
I am able to see these two parts of myself:
the part which leads and the part which
needs direction. These parts reside in
harmony and respect, and I am aware that
these parts become fluid with an overarching
guiding presence of spirit.

It is human nature to think in dualistic terms,
to break ourselves down into object and
subject. Perhaps this is an artificial
dichotomy. In other words, the object and
subject can be one in the same as we work
towards inner balance.

I Enjoy Connection to Everyone in My Heart

When I am in the presence of others, I know that my life is part of a larger life. I am simply a wave in an ocean of being. I know that it is part of a larger life. Through connection, I can appreciate my contribution to others and know in that relatedness, we are more than the sum of all of us.

The Primary Goal of the Human Heart

There are endless philosophies, writings, teachings and schools of therapy to describe and explain the *hows* and *whys* of human existence. They all have one thing in common: survival of the human species.

If we agree that the main goal is to survive, what's next? Most would say it is to be happy; some say it is to be content. I would say it is to create a meaningful philosophy of life.

Tina Chadda, MD

Heartstrings Attach Us

One day, my youngest child asked me what
he should do if we were ever inadvertently
separated. To teach him about attachment, I
came up with the metaphor of "heartstrings."

I explained to him that we are connected by
these invisible strings, from one heart to
another, and should he ever need to reach
me all he had to do was to "pull" on a string.
Now when I pick him up after school each
day, he says, "I knew you would be here. I
pulled on the string!"

Longing to Belong

Each heart longs to belong. Some people are naturally good at belonging. I am not. I have to work at it.

My heart cannot suffer disaffiliation, or not being connected to something larger than myself. Each day I choose to belong with my partner, with my children, with my friends, and with my work. This nourishes and nurtures me. These affiliations are my lifelines and infuse me with life force.

Tina Chadda, MD

Meaning as Connection

I seek the meaning for my life as I go about
the mundane tasks of my life. It is especially
important now, as we seem to be drowning
in an excess of information. I know I have
forgotten about my search when the petty
angers, frustrations and chaos of everyday
life leave behind the residue of futility in the
form of an encompassing hard shell. The
continual search for meaning keeps this shell
protective yet permeable. This means the
negative feelings can easily flow out while I
safeguard the feelings that are precious and
that truly matter. And in doing so, I am
connected with the universe.

Expressing Gratitude to Those Who've Helped You

Gratitude is acknowledging you have received a gift, and being able to recognize the value of the gift and how it affected the way your life unfolded. There is the sense of appreciating the donor's intention and a desire to give back, to return the kindness.

With that in mind, here's how to say thank you: think of someone who was deeply committed to your welfare and selflessly gave to you. Visualize this person before you. Recall the way he spent time with you, the depth of genuine interest he had for you. Be mindful of what you received from this person and what his lasting influence on you has been. Now, imagine seeing him again, and tell him in an honest, open, heartfelt way, "Thank you."

Neela Akasha Ananda

Neela means blue. Akasha is a Sanskrit word that means ether or the essence of the material world, and ananda means bliss in Sanskrit and in other languages as well. Loosley translated, Neela Akasha Ananada means the Blissful Blue Sea of the Infinite Sky. It's a wonderful concept.

Consider the following exercise when you need to feel connected. Sometimes we are accepting of our aloneness and do not wish to speak with anyone. At other moments we feel acutely isolated, thinking that no one has ever experienced what it is that we are experiencing in that singular moment. Do this meditation at those moments, recognizing that the sky is the one visual constant that serves to link us.

Lie down on the grass. Relax your body, and keep your palms facing upwards. Breathe deeply and comfortably. Allow yourself to look all around. See the clouds in their various fluffy shapes. Appreciate the breeze that gently caresses your face. Is the breeze whistling? Are the birds singing? Can you smell the lavender or the roses?

Observe the clouds as they drift across the magnificent, vast sky. Try to "see" the part of the sky obscured by the clouds. Mentally, reach up and touch them. Imagine that these clouds will drift above your neighbor's garden.

Eventually, the clouds will transform themselves into another state. Notice the beautiful blue backdrop to the clouds. Is it bright blue or a grey-blue today? Notice the variations in the color. Say hello to the elegant birds flying high above. Allow your sense of self to merge with something greater than yourself. Let your heart merge with the infinite heart surrounding you. Let yourself feel filled with the expansiveness of the universe. Direct this feeling into your heart. Send a heartfelt greeting to your friends faraway. Know and believe that you are not alone.

When you feel ready, come back to the here and now, and slowly get up. Take that calm, rested, and widened and connected feeling forward through the remainder of your day. Treat it as a wonderful and precious feeling and let it dominate your day.

If the sky is not calm and blue, accept it as it is. Appreciate the beauty that you can see in

it that day. Even a stormy sky with flashes
of lightning has its own magic and mystery.

If it is not possible to be outside to do this,
or if the weather is inclement, then do this
meditation while lying down on the floor.

Connection

Much like your heart pumps vital nutrients throughout your body, connection is what transports love between two people. As we grow more connected to one another, our love strengthens and grows. Connection is often the invisible fabric holding us together. Friedrich Nietzsche said, "Invisible threads are the strongest ties." These are the ones that connect us at an enormously deep level and harmoniously create synchronicity so two hearts can become one.

Without connection, life would be gray, without color. Life would feel cold, and without meaning. Without connection, we would yearn and long for something that was missing from our lives. Connection is the color, the vibrant hues that shine light on otherwise dim corners. It is vivacious and lively, cheerful and spirited, uplifting and inspiring. Without connection we feel lost. But when we become connected, we feel like the path is clear and the journey is worthwhile. Connection starts with the heart and ends with the soul being fully engaged and associated at an enormously high level.

Section Three:
Strength and Healing

*"What happens when people open
their hearts?
They get better."*

Haruki Murakami

Pain is a natural part of life: the loss of a loved one, the grief of a broken heart, the agony of falling short in a personal or professional goal. At some level, we have all experienced a broken heart. But as difficult as it is to be broken, it is even worse if we never stand up, dust ourselves off, and try to put the pieces back together. Healing is the process of reclaiming your fragments and moving forward. It is the opportunity to welcome the light back in, to open our souls and once again feel the warmth, while shedding away the darkness that crept in as the pain overwhelmed.

Healing is an unbelievably natural and therapeutic process, but requires enormous strength and energy. It is easy to discuss, and hard to accomplish. But it is necessary. Without it, we will hold on to the pain, and allow the scars to become a part of us and eventually control and dictate much of our happiness. Healing is the simple act of converting pain into experience; of acknowledging that a negative experience can become a positive learning opportunity if we simply change our vantage point. Healing can push you forward and motivate your growth while inspiring the ability to put one foot in front of the other and welcome what life offers.

Strike a Chord

I will take note of all the feelings that pass
through my heart today. I will acknowledge
even the dissonant ones and not reject them.
Each moment I will link my feelings, trying
to compose myself. I recognize that for this
composition to be melodious I need the
highs and the lows, the good feelings and
the not-so-good ones too. Crescendos and
decrescendos, like the other nuances, are
necessary for a rich, beautiful piece of
music. Therein lies the inherent beauty of all
of my feelings. I will compose myself.

Hidden Jewels in my Heart

I like jewelry. If you get to know me, you'll undoubtedly admire one of my pieces: the coral necklace that I got on the Amalfi Coast one summer, the flower-shaped diamond earrings my children gave me for my birthday, or a gold bangle I was given as part of my wedding ensemble when I was married in India.

What you will never see are the jewels most precious to me. These are the jewels I accumulate in my heart where the ongoing process of alchemical transmutation has turned the base metal of my pain, loss and suffering into gold.

These invisible jewels manifest as my self-discipline, my sense of calm as well as patience, self-compassion and empathy towards others.

Transform Fear into Faith

Without question, fear is the most
challenging emotion that resides in our
hearts. Beware of fear as it confidently takes
you by the hand and takes you for a nice,
long walk on a downward descent.

The practice of transforming fear into faith
restores your strength. Let fear be your fuel.
Sublimate it into faith. Faith is strength.

Meditate on this visual to help you cultivate
faith.

F rantic   **F** ocus
E nvy   **A** wareness
A gitated   **I** ntelligent
R estless   **T** olerant
             H eart-centered

Shift from Fear to Flow

Most of our lives are spent trying to cope with fear of one sort or another. Fear chokes us. Choke is the word that is used when something happens to prevent or interrupt specific flow states.

Here's a helpful way to think about shifting from fear to flow:

F rantic	**F** reedom
E nvy	**L** oving
A gitated	**O** pen
R estless	**W** hole-hearted

How to Use Trauma for Transformation

Trauma, including the constant threat of it, is a fact of life. Everyone experiences it. Trauma can lead to all sorts of post-traumatic states. We hear a lot about this and not enough about the opportunity to use trauma as a way to grow. It's important to understand that trauma in and of itself doesn't make you grow. It sets the stage for growth, and that is what is important.

PTG, or post-traumatic growth, is a new area of study. Doctors, psychologists and psychiatrists are really just starting to learn about it.

Here are the principles for PTG (based on work by Richard Tedeschi and Richard McNally) that I use with myself and my patients:

1) appreciate being alive
2) appreciate increased personal strength
3) appreciate new possibilities that otherwise wouldn't present
4) appreciate relationships more and try to feel closer to others

5) appreciate the role of spirituality in everyday life
6) appreciate that you can make a new lifepath for yourself.

Notice that the foundation for PTG is appreciation or gratitude.

Turn Adversity into Achievement

As soon as you have dealt with the emotional shock of your adverse situation, shift your attention to how you will personally turn things around. This doesn't mean that you have to conclude your time of grieving. In fact, it is likely your feelings and thoughts around this will fluctuate for some time. But in an overall way, start moving your thoughts and emotions towards your new achievement. This will also help you recover from your adversity faster and in a healthier fashion because it gives you a sense of control and an opportunity for mastery.

As you use your adverse circumstances to create achievement, try to create beauty wherever you feel broken, even in the smallest of ways. Make these areas of your life extremely and excruciatingly beautiful. In doing so, the pain, dread and avoidance will dissolve. This does not imply that you forgot those difficult times. This is called personal mastery.

Cell by Cell

Research shows that each day 1% of our cells are replaced. Replacement gives us a chance for betterment. The new cell that replaces the old one can be better. This is incredible, literally, life-changing news.

Cell by cell, I become calm, present, virtuous, strong, healthy and beautiful. Each new cell is brimming with high vibration, love and peace, positivity and optimism. Cell by cell, I create my best self and achieve my life's potential.

My mind is in each cell of my body. I can direct the power of my mind to each cell for its healing and betterment. I can change myself for the better, cell by cell, day by day.

Great thinkers have postulated the idea that belief controls biology, and now science is showing us exactly how this occurs. In particular, neuroscience is revealing how the mind controls the body, and how phenomena like conditioning, the placebo and nocebo effects, and intention work to influence the neural pathways and the release of neurotransmitters from the brain and heart. The emerging field of

neuropsychoanalysis is showing how each
thought, unconscious and conscious, can
have profound influence on us.

Hold -Your-Hurt Heart Meditation

I learned to "hold" my grief or hurt. Here is a simple, effective way to do this.

Lie comfortably on the floor. Breathe mindfully. Place your right hand over your heart area. Allow yourself to acknowledge that your heart is hurting. Visualize your right hand as being comforting and healing. Imagine your hand holding your heart with love, tenderness and reassurance. Train yourself to comfort yourself, just as you would a child. Let your touch be nurturing, gentle and soothing. Do this for several minutes. Be with yourself just as you are at that moment. Being with yourself is soothing yourself. Allow yourself to feel nurtured.

When you feel ready, come back to the here and now, and slowly get up. Take that feeling of self-nurturance forward through the remainder of your day. Treat it as a wonderful and precious feeling and let it dominate your day.

Forgiveness

I have made some mistakes. Some have been small and some have been big.

I forgive myself. I let go. I move on as it's time to be engaged with the world and myself.

(Self) forgiveness can be viewed as a form of (self) love.

Deep Loss as Deepening the Heart

With trauma we are, in an instant, ripped open to the entire universe. There is messy suffering – this part is inevitable. The heart feels torn open. There is the sense of hemorrhaging and fearing that one will exsanguinate.

One day an invitation arrives in the form of another hurt: "You are Invited to a Deepening!" This can be a point of confusion because you thought it was impossible to go any deeper.

I have discovered this invitation is about the deep peace that lies beneath everything else. I have trained myself to attend these invitations, especially when I am not in the mood. Simply tolerating your conditions is healing and will make you stronger.

Letting Go

Letting go is not a form of passivity or giving up. In fact, it's far from giving up. The term itself could be interpreted as implying no work, but it is work. It is an active act of surrender of resistance towards freedom for the heart.

Here is an example of letting go in my life and it's not an uncommon story: my first three children were created with the help of modern medicine. A few years later when all of the baby paraphernalia had been given away and I felt my family was complete, I discovered I was pregnant! In retrospect I could see that my "letting go," or surrender, of the overwhelming, all-consuming desire for a pregnancy "freed up" my body for the initially desired experience.

The Most Important Thing You'll Ever Do

The most important thing you can do for yourself is to help yourself. This may seem obvious to you. It wasn't always to me.

One day, as I strolled down a lovely little street called Tranby Avenue, I came across a stack of books on the sidewalk outside of number 24. On top of the books was a handwritten note that said, "Help Yourself." I did exactly what the note said. I took all the books. And although I enjoyed the books immensely, the deepest value came from the message in the note:

"Help Yourself."

The image of that note with those two simple words forged itself in my mind. It was probably because I was broken, and when you are broken you start to search for that which will repair you.

Start helping yourself, and keep helping yourself. Starting to help yourself is the first step in building strength. Never stop developing your strength.

Psychic Immunity

When I exercise, I am strengthening my physical immunity. I feel full of energy and my stamina is great. Viruses and bacteria do not easily make me ill. My appetite is good and I sleep well.

When I meditate, I am boosting my psychic immunity by developing my inner-self. My mood is more even and stable, and I become more resilient. I can handle the small setbacks of everyday life with poise and I don't take them too seriously. And my relationships are enriched.

Strength and Healing

Accepting that pain is part of life is also the act of accepting the notion that healing is a natural and necessary response to the occurrence of pain. Thus, it is only natural to strive towards beginning the healing process. But that may only be possible after we grieve and cope with the initial onset of excruciating pain.

If we do not begin to heal, then we will continue to swim in the agony of the pain. We will trade happiness for sadness, good times for bad ones, and standing still for the opportunity to grow. Pain is inevitable. Often times, it is unavoidable. To truly love requires the acceptance that at the end of the road, pain may be waiting. But recognize the trade-off as a worthwhile endeavor. All the great times should never be clouded by the pain at the end of the journey.

Accept pain and begin to heal. Only then can you truly continue your journey to a positive and successful life.

Section Four: Mindfulness

"The present moment is filled with joy and happiness. If you are attentive, you will see it."

Thích Nhất Hạnh

Mindfulness is the process of being fully present in the moment. It includes the ability to radiate outwards from your heart. Here is how I do this: I close my eyes and breathe mindfully from my heart-center. I access the feeling of love, then mentally radiate it outward in concentric circles. The circles fill my heart, then my entire being. I continue in this fashion outwards to my family, my neighborhood, and community. I let the circles continue out into the universe.

These circles encompass the ability to be mindful of friends, family, loved ones, and all other beings in this world. It is the glow that resonates within and often times covers those that stand close. Being mindful of others and respectful towards them allows you to be fully engaged in the moment and dedicated to building a heartfelt and connected relationship. You can then be connected in this warm, enveloping energy field to everyone on this planet.

Giftwaves in my Heart

Precious giftwaves are stored in the library of my heart-mind. Giftwaves are the ever-growing and accumulated pool of teachings and energies from my dear teachers: my beloved childhood schoolteachers, university professors, medical supervisors and preceptors, my life coach, my meditation and yoga teachers, my psychoanalyst, my guru, and my mentor. I am deeply fond of each of them.

I regularly call upon these masters and their giftwaves for knowledge and wisdom, inspiration and guidance. They are always here. Through mental attention and visualizing them before me, I have access to them wherever I am. What an incredible gift!

Studying the Hurt in Your Heart Meditation

It's extremely useful if you can learn to study whatever it is that hurts your heart. This gives you a mechanism for the constant repair and care of your heart. As you master this meditation, you will be able to better soothe yourself. Do this from a less attached, or detached, position.

Visualize this: stand comfortably and breathe mindfully. Now imagine placing your hurt on a table. Lay it there gently. Now take a step back, and slowly walk around the table. As you do so, see the various aspects of the situation, being careful not to favor one view. Allow yourself to see various sides. Say to yourself, "Ah! There are many ways to see this." Walk around the table a few times. Note what you learn about the situation and yourself. As you wrap up, say a mental "thank you" for this learning opportunity.

My Heart-Mind

I know that the intelligence of my heart-mind works in perfect harmony with my brain-mind to create the wisdom I need. My clear mind and feeling heart are complementary partners and do not conflict. I look for solutions to my challenges within this space of wisdom.

There is a critical distinction between intellect and intelligence. As Joseph Chilton Pearce so beautifully describes, intellect refers to and involves the brain whereas intelligence refers to and involves the heart. He likens the intellect to the "masculine" side of our being and intelligence to the "feminine" side. The intellect is that part which is concerned with linear analytic concepts like math and science. Intelligence is the other part that has to do with intuition, a sense of wholeness and oneness, wisdom, well-being, permanence and the survival of the planet.

Our higher intelligence results from this mix of intellect and intelligence. The tension between these polarities, the mind and the heart, gives rise to creativity. However, we live in a time where there is a huge split between the mind and the heart, the intellect and the intelligence. This split between the heart and mind thwarts and threatens our development. The more we can merge our heart and head, the more fully and deeply we can experience the richness of life.

Fully Present with My Whole Heart

I choose to fully live life in the here and now. I am in this moment, with my whole entire being. To do any less would mean that I am not fully living and not enjoying life at its fullest. If I do not give things my full attention, then I cannot enjoy the fullness of my life.

I live and create my life moment by moment. Each moment holds instruction for me. My job is to discover that instruction. It is in this awareness, that each moment can teach me something, that I am able to grow and develop.

A Stranger to Myself

This may sound strange, but it works and it's very helpful.

On purpose, I sometimes pretend I am a stranger in my own life and that I have just stepped into my existence. Where did that cushion on the sofa come from? Are these plates new? I love these new shoes!

All seems new and fresh from this perspective. It is a way to liberate myself from any apparent mundaneness and familiarity. In this way, I get to notice things and feelings that I, perhaps, have neglected. I have a chance to see what is still mysterious in the familiar. And I see the blessings in my life that I normally take for granted. Thus, I am alleviated from being alienated from my own heart.

Heart as Entry Point to the Present

My heart can beat only in this moment and I am therefore reminded to be in the present. Whenever I wander off to the past or future, I simply remind myself that my heartbeat is now.

Mindfulness

The first part of the word mindfulness is mind. That is no coincidence. The mind plays an important role in connecting us to everything around us. Once we concentrate on that which is in front of us, we can begin the simple yet meaningful act of building a connection. Being mindful leads to being connected and being connected leads to the nourishment of love within relationships.

Without mindfulness, there can be diminished meaning. You can feel disjointed and disconnected. Through mindful awareness of others, you begin the exchange of an important level of mutual respect that is the foundation and one of the pillars for successful relationships. Be lost in the moment. Turn down the noise that often surrounds your life and welcome in the silence and clarity that only manifests when you focus and are mindful.

Section Five: Reflection

"Life can only be understood backwards; but it must be lived forwards."

Søren Kierkegaard

Reflection is a powerful opportunity. But many times, it is a lost one. We rarely take the appropriate and necessary time to simply evaluate and analyze an experience. Big or small, each and every action and experience impacts the course of our lives. In fact, our lives are the culmination of each of these actions.

But consider how often you take the time after a busy day and think through your daily experiences. How often do you truly reflect? Being mindful of your ability to reflect is the first step. The next step is acknowledging that there is enormous power in scheduling the time to evaluate the breadcrumbs that are left behind. Only then can you reach your true destination.

Heart-Vessel as Faith

I often think of my heart as a vessel for
faith, not just blood. It's impossible for me
to pour water into a glass without first
believing that I can do this, and second, that
the glass can contain the water. In other
words, pouring water is an act of faith.

Faith is a mental continuum that requires at
the outset, a small belief in something
significant. The awakening of faith is the
hardest step. Then you just get on the
continuum and it builds on itself.

You might be thinking faith is what a
desperate person takes to. But what if you
come to see how precious something is?

These Words are Living Tissue, Not Fossil

Treat these words (as long as they are acceptable to you) that I have pulled out from my heart and brain as living tissue, not fossil. Each letter and each word is a drop of life. Breathe these words into yourself as you read, incorporating them into your being so that they become your living and breathing tissue.

This is how to really "take it in." You can do this with anything: a book, a meditation, or a piece of music or artwork. Experience whatever is before you with sincerity, let it penetrate your being by mentally breathing it into yourself.

The Virtuous Heart

Some days I have to remind myself of the virtues, and nurture the ones that I feel are lacking in me.

It's not enough to simply weed the garden; the soil must be turned and fertilized, and the sun must shine enough for the flowers and plants to flourish. We are no different. It's not enough to simply remove the obstacles that thwart our progress; we need to actively create conditions for our best development. Planting virtues into the heart-mind helps to create the positive mental states that we need in order to grow. You can read the next meditation to learn how to do this.

Throughout the ages mankind has cherished these virtues: creativity, courage, friendship, judgment, love of learning, perspective, honesty, curiosity, valor, love, kindness, social intelligence, zest, forgiveness, humility, fairness, leadership, collegiality, humor, sincerity, vigor, hope, gratitude, heroism, moderation, appreciation of beauty, prudence, excellence, self-regulation, humanity, and spirituality.

Using Meditation to Cultivate Character

Our character is the core, or heart, of our being. Have you ever wished for a different heart? Are there qualities you would like to have or has someone important in your life told you to change?

We've all had that experience. We can all change if we choose to. Change isn't the only motivation to cultivate virtues within each of us. Modern day resilience training is really about virtue training.

Clearly, we each have our own reason for wanting to "upgrade" our heart.

Here's a beautiful way to bring a new character trait into you and to grow it: visualize a model who best exhibits the virtue you want to bring into yourself. See your model manifesting the desired virtue in a few different scenarios. Place your visual into a bubble, mentally direct it above you, then take it into your heart-center, allowing it to dissolve within you. Continue to breathe mindfully and with each breath let the virtue emanate throughout your heart until your heart is overflowing with this virtue. Then treat this virtue as your best trait going forward. Do this every day until you have mastered the desired virtue, then move on to the next one.

Understanding Your Emotions

The (biological) goal of life is to survive.
The brain is an organ built for social
survival. The mind – comprised of the brain
and all related-organizing and processing
functions – is then a survival mechanism.
Emotions themselves are what the mind uses
to help us survive.

A helpful way to really understand feelings
or emotion is this definition of emotion:
energy in motion.

The emotional goal of life is to overcome
fear and become happy. We have to
sufficiently overcome fear in order to be
happy. But because we spend most of our
lives coping with fear, it's challenging to
experience more than fleeting happiness.

Dark Times

Each of us goes through very difficult
periods in life.

When we are in the middle of our darkness,
we feel alone – like we are the only person
on earth who has ever suffered in this way.
These periods are painful, dreadful, and
intense. Time slows, making each moment
last a long time. However, when things are
good, time flies.

All you can do is let that time pass. Let
yourself cry. Do your best to learn from it.
Let yourself receive comfort from the people
around you. Ask for help, and help yourself,
if even in the smallest ways.

From the Outside to the Inside

What makes us really change? What makes our heart grow?

External life events that we perceive as difficult or traumatic are usually the catalyst for internal change. Death of a loved person or pet, sudden significant loss of some type, or an illness like cancer makes people more contemplative. We are forced to consider larger and more important life issues at such junctures and we can use these times as opportunity for increasing our sense of spirituality.

Each Day I am Birthed in my Heart

I was born in my body complete and perfect as an infant. Now, my physical body has stopped growing. Over the course of linear time, I grew up and accumulated a breadth of experience, and I will continue to do so.

It is in my heart where another dimension of growth exists. A new aspect of every experience is given birth there each day. It is up to me to regularly acknowledge this. This process allows me to develop depth of experience. In this way I enjoy and reap the benefits of the breadth and depth of my life experience.

Reflection

Each past day offers us a powerful opportunity to grow through reflection. And each new one offers us that same opportunity to begin the process all over again. Even one day without reflection can have an impact on the ability to live a prosperous life. Take the time to reflect each and every day. Don't let an opportunity to improve yourself and reconnect with your heart and soul pass.

At night I rest in the womb of my heart. Here, I am assured softness, comfort, and love – all which serve to renew and rejuvenate me. I can begin tomorrow fresh.

What a relief that each day offers a fresh start, a new beginning.

Section Six: Self-Inquiry

"Self-inquiry is simple. It does not require you to do anything, change anything, think anything, or understand anything. It only asks you to pay careful attention to what is true and real."

Arijuda Ardagh

True reflection is grounded in the notion that you are willing to dive deep into your heart and soul through honest and unbiased self-inquiry. It is not always easy to acknowledge your weaknesses and is certainly difficult to evaluate where you could improve on a personal level. Thus, self-inquiry requires a strong will and desire to adjust and progress.

Generally, we are not pre-wired to respond in this manner. No one wants to admit they could have done better. But when we can, the result is greater potential for growth. Our heart beats as our mind flourishes. Thus, to self-reflect and inquire is to welcome the occasion to develop and expand our hearts, minds, and souls.

How to Affirm Yourself

Each morning make it your habit to practice an affirmation. "Affirmation" derives from the Latin *affirmare*, meaning "to strengthen or make steady."

An affirmation is a positive statement that you say to yourself. You can also think of it as a self-promise. Treat the affirmation as a living, dynamic, breathing entity, not a static declaration or a statement. Your affirmation has a life of its own. As you practice it, you will be giving it life and in this process it becomes part of your being. It will become part of you, and part of your cells, and your cellular memory.

When you have finished getting ready to go to work in the morning, and after you have done your makeup or put on your tie, stand in front of the mirror in a private spot and take a moment to be in touch with the essence of yourself before you turn your attention to the rest of the world.

Because we can only look into one eye at a time, do the affirmation twice. This is key: say the affirmation once looking into your right eye, and again while looking into your left eye. Repeat the affirmation mid-day and in the late afternoon, because that's how fragile our self-love, and our healthy narcissism is.

Stand up straight and tall in front of a mirror. Take yourself seriously. Breathe mindfully. Direct your breath to the words, and give them life. Say to yourself (something like this) each morning: "My life is sacred. I can access the strength to handle absolutely anything that will come my way today. Peace and calm are with me."

Take this feeling of being strengthened and steadied forward through the day. Train yourself to let that feeling predominate.

Pressure is My Partner in Growth

When I am stressed I tell myself that pressure is my partner in growth. The emotional, and sometimes even physical, sensation of pressure means that I am expanding. I remind myself that something is trying to be born, or even surface.

I work with, not against, myself. I gently encourage myself and do not push.

My heart strives to choose growth over regression, rejection or stagnation. I feel alive with the sense of pressure, this life force. As long as my heart is beating, I want to feel alive.

From a neuroendocrine point of view, the brain cannot distinguish between fear and excitement. So before you conclude that pressure will crush you, tolerate the pressure and try saying: "Pressure is my partner in growth, pressure is my partner in growth…" And then repeat.

A is for Attitude

I am learning to always go for an "A" in the course on Attitude. The reason for this is that everything depends on it.

Here's how to cultivate a heart-centered attitude each morning before you face the world: assess yourself, paying particular attention to your mood and energy. Focus on your self-regard and anticipate your needs during the day. Create an internal environment of safety, peace and love that protects you. Increase your vibrational frequency. Go give your best self to the world and expect the best in return.

Self-Acceptance

I accept my life circumstances as they are and I accept myself exactly as I am. I do this despite and because of the imperfections or faults. I try not to feel inferior or defective in any way. I self-monitor for negation, criticism, and inadequate feelings. Mindful of my faults, I do not let them become my neuroses.

I am on a constant search for a higher level of experience, bliss and harmony. I am aware at times of my lack of self-acceptance which wears me down, taking me to a lower level of existence where I am prone to feeling unhappy and stressed. I don't want to ruin the wonderful inherent potential with which I am blessed. I have learned that things can shift when there is more self-acceptance in the presence of the desire for self-improvement. I believe the essence of the idea is to aspire to improve but not become preoccupied with that.

Meditation as Mediation

We meditate for all sorts of reasons: to have calm and peace, to increase creativity, to lateralize the left and right brain hemispheres, to improve health, and to increase mental clarity.

Another way to think about meditation is that it offers you a space to conduct a mediation with yourself. We are often immersed in our own conflicting dialogues. Meditation provides a space to conduct that discussion but in a way that is less inherently adversarial.

Meaning and Mindfulness in the Heart

The average life is an accumulation of residue from past crises. As a result, we spend most of our life regretting the past and fearing the future. We can change this in a very simple way, and it's something we do in small ways in our everyday life without being fully aware of it.

Here's how to handle a challenging past-experience: give the event a different meaning. What's happened has happened – you can't change that. The only variable you can control is the meaning. In changing the meaning, you have the power to make the otherwise unpalatable palatable.

In my work with patients who have terminal illnesses, the therapy usually revolves around a search for what can provide the most meaning. One woman, a 45 year-old software engineer with a brain tumor, decided to quit her job and travel as much as she could with her young children and husband. That she was able to create a bank of loving family memories for her children gave her tremendous pleasure and meaning.

I know that her entire family deeply appreciated her stance.

Viktor Frankl said it best in his book *Man's Search for Meaning*: "...the last of human freedoms – to choose one's attitude in any given set of circumstances, to choose one's own way."

Appreciative Inquiry

I once took a business class. Here's what I learned:

When organizations re-structure, they use a philosophy known as appreciative inquiry. The underlying thinking is that sometimes it's better to appreciate what's good rather than seeking out and solving problems. It's a positive thinking-based way to evaluate the situation and create healthy energy and action for change. Each key person in the organization is asked to reflect on the things that work when the organization is most alive, productive and successful.

You can engage in your own appreciative inquiry by asking these questions. What are the pivotal factors that help to facilitate this? Then, more fully awaken to these factors and appreciate them!

You can apply appreciative inquiry in your own life. For example, if you are feeling unproductive, inquire as to the conditions when you are most productive, and then try to re-create those circumstances.

Self-Inquiry

It is not easy to proactively survey your
DNA. Your heart and soul have an
enormous impact on your life. Through self-
inquiry and then self-adjustment, you
position yourself to grow and mature as a
person. In each of us lie many strengths and
strong qualities. But amongst the good, there
may be a small grouping of qualities and
characteristics that could be improved and
enhanced. Only through self-inquiry can we
connect to those fibers and recognize the
need to enrich these areas.

No one lives a perfect life. We can all do
better and become more valuable members
of humanity. Our hearts intimately connect
us to the world around us. Thus, the stronger
your heart, the more connected and linked
you will find yourself. On a daily basis, take
the time to reflect and inquire into your
strengths and weaknesses, successes and
failures, and your heart and soul. The result
will only be one that is positive.

Section Seven: Spirituality

"Understand spirituality not as some kind of religious dogma or ideology but as the domain of awareness where we experience values like truth, goodness, beauty, love and compassion, and also intuition, creativity, insight and focused attention."

Deepak Chopra

Spirituality is the amazingly powerful link between your inner heart and an outward spirit. That spirit could be anything. What is important is that there is a strong belief in something bigger than the self. When compared to the notion of spirit, the self is a seemingly small part of humanity. But the relationship between self and spirit is a powerful connection, one that transcends worldly desires and is something much bigger than each of us.

Spirituality is oneness. It is the act of believing in a guiding force, a shining light, that both leads us through challenges and directs us through obstacles. Spirituality heals pain and lifts us up when we cannot rise on our own. The belief in something greater allows each of us to relinquish control and rely upon our spiritual connection to ensure we arrive safely at our destination. Spirituality offers us the exciting opportunity to believe in something greater than and will ultimately offer the hope and direction we need to both survive and prosper.

What The Universal Heart Seeks

The greatest challenge of the human heart is to overcome the sense of separateness. In everyday life this translates to the ever-present feeling that something is missing. That feeling is also called loneliness, depression, and anxiety. All are states of emotional cut-off.

The universal heart seeks a sense of being non-separate, a sense of connection, peace and fulfillment.

Turning the Heart as Orientation

I turn my heart towards myself, then my
partner, my children and my family. I turn
my heart towards my community, my work
and towards the universe.

I must turn my heart to the other before I can
truly open myself, optimizing my capacity
to receive goodwill and love from others. I
can orient myself in this direction. I allow
God to assist me in my orientation each day.

My Steadfast Heart

I choose to be steady within my heart. The light-beams of the universe keep me steady and strong so that I remain focused in my mind.

God in My Heart

Here is an easy and accessible way to understand the concept of God.

God is that part of my reality that brings out the best in me during my worst time.

When I Pray

When I pray, I pray with all my heart and all my soul.

Otherwise, I don't bother.

God is in Me – I am God

God is in me and inside of me. I am in God and inside of God.

It is the feeling of "in-ness" without distinction of God and me. And therefore I am God and you are God.

Praying is One of the Hardest Things I Have Ever Done

Learning to pray and meditate as an adult with sincerity and concentration is perhaps one of the most difficult things I have ever done. As a private experience, prayer can be deeply moving and life shaping.

Each day I look forward to this time in prayer. With practice, I am able to cultivate a sense of calm. I set aside this time to manage my everyday anxieties.

I have learned that I cannot survive without this peace. I need this peace in order to thrive, and I choose to thrive on this earth.

Heaven, Earth, and Everything
in Between

It is in my heart where I hold heaven, earth
and everything in between. Here, in this part
of me, I will find my divine-self, my earth-
self and other parts of myself. These other
parts are not cut off, they are simply
evolving and finding where they fit and
connect with everything else.

Tina Chadda, MD

One Way to Pray

This is a simple way to pray.

Sit comfortably. Close your eyes and
breathe mindfully. Let yourself drop into
your body. Imagine a gentle, warm light all
around you. With the in-breath, bring the
light into your body. Breathe this light
through all parts of your body. Do this for
several minutes.

In this prayer you are actually working on
bringing your mind and body together, and
promoting harmony and well-being.

What is Holy in the Heart?

Holiness is the quality someone or something has that helps humans achieve their potential for becoming fully human. Attributes of others, experiences and places can be holy in that they fulfill this function.

Tina Chadda, MD

Feelings are Angels

I came across this while sitting in synagogue
one day at the Bat Mitzvah of a dear friend's
daughter. These words really touched my
heart, and I hope they touch yours too:

Angels are another name for feelings.
When we love and act with kindness
we create angels of love and kindness.
When we hate and act with violence
we create angels of hatred and violence.
It is our job to fill our world with angels of
love: messengers of kindness that link
people together as one family.

My Heart has Infinite Capacity

Just when I think my heart can't take anything more it does.

My heart exploded with love after the birth of my first child and I assumed I wouldn't be able to feel the same kind of exquisite love for another child. But when my second child was born, my heart exploded and expanded again. The same thing occurred when my next two children were born.

Learning that my heart could expand like this felt like discovering a wonderful, fundamental secret.

Why didn't someone tell me that would happen?

Desired events bring good or positive feelings and represent a state of expansion. We can easily accommodate these experiences into our hearts. Undesired events, like everyday disappointments or bigger traumas, bring negative feelings and a sense of contraction; we might even feel like we are dying.

Expansion-states are life-giving while contraction-states are life-depleting.

However, it is in the very expansion of the heart, that we are able to cope with the contracted states. In other words, sometimes we can't tell the difference. Our hearts are able to accommodate everything in an infinite fashion.

Loss and Spirituality

Deep loss can offer you a spiritual heart. We could even say that deep loss or pain is necessary for spiritual inquiry.

Life is a series of ascending spirals (of success) and descending spirals (of strife). When we're busy going up, we're not too concerned with why, but when we're going down, WHY dominates.

Loss can be an actual loss, not getting what you want or aimed for, an illness or a death of a loved one. Loss can also be just realizing that what gave you meaning earlier can no longer do that. Another kind of loss is when we retire or age.

My Heart Grows in the Direction
of the Sun

My heart is subject to the heliotropic effect.
Just as the earth's flowers and plants need
sunlight to grow, I need to be nurtured and
nourished by a sun-God. My heart is like a
bud, and the petals are tightly drawn in. The
awareness of something greater than myself
allows me to unfold, blossom and eventually
bloom to reach my human potential. I
choose to grow tall and strong, beautiful and
free, like a sunflower.

If you do not believe in God you can benefit
from the human heliotropic effect through a
relationship with a teacher or role model, or
simply by surrounding yourself with
positive people and experiences.

The vast fields of incredibly beautiful
golden sunflowers in Umbria, Italy is a
favorite image for me. Captivated by the
majestic stature of the sunflowers, I was
compelled to learn more about the
heliotropic effect. Sunflowers clearly
capitalize on the heliotropic effect, and so
can we.

It turns out that there is a human heliotropic effect. The concept that all living systems, including humans, lean toward that which is life-giving and positive, rather than negative, comes from the field of positive leadership. The benefits of a positive environment range from ordinary enhancement, to success, to great success – a phenomenon now called flourishing.

Release Resistance

In my heart I strive to release the small
resistances that hold me back each day. As I
release the resistance, I feel free and God
can guide me. When the resistances melt
away, I recognize the presence of God.

Your Heart's Passion

Following your heart's passion allows you
to enter what's called a flow state. This is
when you become fully absorbed into an
activity and the rest of the world falls away.
It is as if another energy overtakes. A pure
love and life energy seems to emanate from
the heart itself.

Indeed, it is cosmic energy flowing through
you. This permits us full engagement with
the self and the universe.

Some of us experience flow at work, while
playing a musical instrument, during a
sports activity or during sex. Meditation and
prayer also promote this state of being,
which enhances overall well-being.

I Seek to Refine my Heart

I ask for guidance to remove the impurities
and blocks from my heart-soul so that
energy flows freely through me, keeping me
connected to everything and everyone
around me. As long as such impurities are
present, I know that I will suffer isolation
and loneliness and my creativity will be
impeded.

The Lonely Heart

The major ingredient in loneliness that poses difficulty is fear. Learning to cope with this is necessary. We are really never alone. The solitude of suffering can make us feel alone – going through dark periods in our lives where we are dealing with terrible circumstances and challenges. It's helpful to know that each human being goes through this period. The sheer knowledge of this can keep one alive. Reminding oneself of this prevents complete alienation from the self. Sometimes you see people who have, through a series of circumstances, become completely cut off from the core of the self.

Spirituality

Within the realm of human and divine communication is ultimately where the self can relate and believe in something larger than the self. It is through this special and sacred communication where one can listen to God and receive guidance and support through times in need. Spirituality is the experience of believing in something greater, something more powerful, something that can uplift and inspire when needed.

Take the time to develop your spirituality. There is no roadmap to becoming spiritual. But it does require belief and a genuine desire to connect with something greater. Nurture your spirit and welcome spirituality into your life.

Section Eight: Heart

"The best and most beautiful things in the world cannot be seen or even touched – they must be felt with the heart."

Helen Keller

The heart is the universal symbol for what it means to be human. Life itself is defined by the presence of a heartbeat; it's possible to be brain-dead but as long as there is a detectable heartbeat, it is said that life is present.

Throughout history the heart has represented different things to different people: the location of soul and consciousness, the seat of emotion and humanity, erotic love and passion, ethical or moral functions, special insights or cognitive powers, emotion, intellect, wisdom, the divine, warmth and compassion, virtue and value, will, and even identity.

Whatever functions you ascribe to your symbolic heart, these define the core, or the essence, of what you believe yourself to be.

Atha and The Ambivalent Heart

Atha is the very first word in the Patanjali Yoga Sutras. It literally means "now" and it encompasses the notion of an inward readiness and commitment. In other words, atha encourages us to work through our ambivalence, and decide and commit in the "now." Commitment is key. The reason for this is that commitment itself provides a grounding energy and framework. It provides stability and structure. Ambivalence, on the other hand, is unsteady and uncertain.

To practice atha means that in each moment we must choose where we want to live. Our life is simply strung-together moments of time from the past, present, and future. So the word atha can also be seen as an invitation to select your vantage point. Implicit in this is the notion of looking at things from a new, fresh angle each day, which can only be done in the "now" or the present moment.

Atha is about acceptance whereas ambivalence is about wondering how things might otherwise be. Letting things be as they are in the now is powerful. Acceptance means openness to newness, which is about growth, healing and transformation.

Embedded in the term atha is the idea of the heart-mind. We are invited in each moment to approach with a fresh, or beginner's heart-mind, to all that we come in contact with. Be curious. Be interested. Be aware. Let go of the past. Let go of ideas that no longer are accurate. Let go of maladaptive patterns.

Being in the now allows for the new, which is required for renewal and growth of life. When you are in the now and practicing atha, you cannot be ambivalent.

What Rules: Sattva

I strive towards cultivating a sattvic heart-
mind of love and compassion, intelligence, a
sense of rightness, purity and harmony,
nonviolence, balance, virtue, flexibility,
temperance and wisdom. Refining my heart-
mind and remaining appropriately detached
helps me to focus on the greater good.

Sattva comes from yoga psychology and it
has to do with values that are universally
accepted to be positive and good.

The Science of Tears

I cried on and off for a handful of years
following the loss of my home.
Retrospectively, I can say I cried more than
I care to remember. For a period of time,
when the act of crying itself made me feel
inadequate and inferior, I would force
myself to stop crying.

Crying a little bit everyday helped to release
the tension, and usually my heart would feel
better and lighter afterwards. I later learned
that humans apparently are the only species
to produce emotional tears, as opposed to
natural tears, which occur when our eyes are
irritated or require lubrication. Mostly tears
are made up of water, salt, and some
antibodies and antibacterial enzymes.
Emotional tears have other ingredients
including prolactin, adrenocorticotropic and
leucine encephalin, a natural painkiller. For
this reason we can feel better after a good
cry.

The Heart of Duhkha

Duhkha literally means "bad space" and in the heart-mind it is experienced as hurt, pain or suffering.

At the heart of duhkha lies an opportunity for self-discovery. You can try to look at your suffering from all possible angles before you take any further action. Being aware of all the possibilities lets you make choices that will cause less negativity. You can also consider what happened in the first place and try to prevent those conditions from arising again in the future.

Sometimes we can anticipate suffering. The awareness of it may allow us to avoid it or minimize the associated pain. The awareness reveals information about ourselves.

Buddhist philosophy suggests four steps to decreasing suffering:

1. Clearly identify the symptoms of the pain.
2. Name the cause.
3. Set an intention to eradicate the cause.
4. Activate your intention.

Reconciliation

I recognize there are disparate, polarized parts of myself within my heart-soul. I will allow these parts to be reconciled so that I can exist in a state of harmony, not disharmony. I choose to be strong and united within myself.

Keep Wonder Alive

Wonder must be kept alive within the heart.
Descartes classified wonder as the first of
the six passions of the soul.

The insights provided by wonder are
endless. Wonder keeps us attuned to the
world and to the deepest part of ourselves.
The feeling of wonder prevents us from
feeling defeated in everyday life and lets us
feel alive and joyful. The emotional and
intellectual pursuit of daily wonder allows
for constant perceptual awareness.

I Direct My Heart

Before I meditate I must direct my heart.

I view my heart as the locus of my emotion and intellect. So, before I meditate I turn my mind inward. I can concentrate through this inward state of mind and being, allowing my intensity of thought and emotion to build. It is through this, then, that my awareness builds.

The Landscape Within My Heart

Whenever I feel frustrated or restless, or when I feel the pressure to escape such human emotions, I go to the serene and peaceful landscape within my heart. I can access this beauty and calm whenever I feel the need, no matter where I am. Unlike the external world, even at the edges and ledges of my heart, I know I can find comfort.

The Words I Place Upon My Heart

I choose the words I place upon my heart
with great care. I am learning that each
word, with each breath, gradually penetrates
all of the layers of my heart. The words then
become part of my living tissue, and part of
what I send back out to the universe.

Heart Energy is Bliss

The human body has energy fields. This has been known for thousands of years but still isn't fully accepted by conventional medicine. These fields are self-organizing patterns and extend beyond the physical body, linking us to the environment and to others. Our energy fields are an invisible extension of ourselves. Our bodies and our hearts can absorb energy from other fields.

Everything is energy, and it's basically either positive or negative. Things in the environment, like other people, influence the quality of the energy. See if you can be in touch with your own energy by trying to sense or intuit it with your body, not brain-mind. Open up to your heart-center and access the wonderful blissful energy that flows from there. Allow yourself to access the bliss inside. Take in the beauty and passion, and try not to absorb negative energy.

The Angry Heart

Anger is a highly charged emotion. In other words, anger has a huge amount of energy behind it. That's what fuels us when we have an "outburst" or a "tantrum." Anger ranges from mild irritation, all the way to murderous rage. At a societal level, it takes the form of riots and killings.

Don't be afraid of your anger. You will be alright so long as you can sublimate the immense power of it in a useful way.

Ordinary, uncomplicated anger is about unmet needs. The easiest and quickest way to deal with anger in your heart is to simply acknowledge its presence and then to use the energy behind it in a positive way. Practically speaking, ask yourself, "What need do I have right now that is not being met?" This way you end up doing or creating something beneficial, and you release yourself from being enslaved to the anger.

My Heart is My Anchor

I turn to my heart-mind and soul when my brain-mind is flooded with thoughts. There is always an anchor in my heart; my heart is my anchor. It is a quiet place of stillness. I rely on this sense of permanence within myself in a transient, fluid and impermanent material world.

My Heart's Intention

Here is an example of how to set your
intention each morning before you meditate.
The intention has two parts to it: the first
part says something about the content of the
intention and the second part is about the
process you will be immersing yourself in as
you set about fulfilling the content.

Here's what I say to myself: "This process is
about awakening. I make a promise to
myself to concentrate and make every
moment count."

My Heart Elevates Me

By increasing the vibrational frequency of
the heart through prayer, meditation,
affirmation, or music we can elevate our
sense of being. In fact, the effect can be
profound. As you increase your heart's
vibrational frequency, you will become
more powerful in comforting and loving
others.

Our Hearts have Common Interests

Our ideas may differ, and this happens frequently. But in our hearts, we often have much more in common with others than we can ever imagine: fear, anxiety, grief, hope, and joy. In this way, we are more like-hearted than like-minded.

We can be like-minded, but ultimately it is what is in our hearts that will determine if we can stay together or not.

Could it be so Simple as Looking in My Heart?

Sometimes my thoughts become excessive and complicated, and I recognize that I may be misidentifying these intellectual artifacts as my reality. But I know my reality is much greater than this, and that awareness is larger than my brain-mind.

I remind myself to access my heart-intelligence in order to heighten awareness. It is the combination of brain and heart intelligence then that gives me access to cosmic intelligence.

Essential from the Nonessential

It is my heart-mind that can immediately distinguish what is essential for my survival and what I can discard. My brain-mind rationalizes and intellectualizes excessively at times. My heart seems to cut through it all and I get my answer. What an incredible relief this is. I am consistently amazed with the power of my heart-mind.

My Heart is the Most Sensitive Detector

Emotion is much faster than thought. My heart detects wordless nuances of the world around me. Why am I surprised? After all, my heart gave me life and sustains my life. I understand the built-in detector function to be part of my heart's life-support functions. It is fundamental to my survival.

Scientifically speaking, this is how the heart can know something before the brain.

Passion in My Heart

When I feel listless, I look within my heart
to be reminded of my passions and
pleasures. I am reminded of all the things
that nourish me and fuel me to pursue my
life of productivity and abundance.

Ideation in My Heart

I am delighted by the new ideas I sometimes
discover within my heart. I am reassured of
the presence of creation within myself.
There is so much to look forward to.

Economy of the Heart

In the outside world money is our currency for the everyday exchanges in life. Dollars and cents are the driving force for the economy of commerce.

In the heart, gratitude is the currency. It is the lifeline within the self, to others, and to the divine. Gratitude as an emotion has a way of "cutting through" in the heart. It creates a regenerative effect emotionally, spiritually, mentally, and perhaps even physically.

Gratitude resonates at a high vibrational frequency, creating a magnetic effect within your being, thereby attracting the magnificent life.

Heartfelt Thanksgiving

We all have difficult crossings and journeys. These are the experiences that we struggle through while enduring pain. We are either forced on such journeys or we choose them. The completion of such a season in the heart brings sublime joy and peace.

Recall such a time in your life. Visualize it before you. Remember the challenging feelings you experienced during that time. Then bring to mind the triumph you felt afterwards. Focus on that joy. Allow the feelings of victory to envelop you. Finally, express heartfelt thanks to the universe.

Heart Chakra Meditation

This visualization meditation focuses on bringing prana into your heart and opening up your heart-center. It's a good exercise when you are feeling tight, or when you feel somewhat lifeless or listless. In the beginning, you will notice your resistance. With practice this will melt away. Mentally think of the prana as vital nectar, or the most expensive, delicious wine you've ever had.

Sit comfortably in the meditation posture on the floor or sit comfortably on a chair. Begin to breathe mindfully. Now imagine a wide, transparent tube going into the center of your chest or into your heart. Train yourself to understand that there is no other "end" to the tube. As you inhale, mentally bring prana into you. Draw in love, compassion, and softness. Give nothing away when you exhale. Continue to breathe slowly, and repeat this. Allow the prana to bring unconditional love into your heart-center. Allow yourself to feel truly alive and appreciate the tingling throughout your entire body. Continue doing this for several minutes until you feel you prana has reached all parts of your body.

When you feel ready, come back to the here and now and slowly get up. Take that feeling of vital aliveness forward through the remainder of your day. Treat it as a wonderful and precious feeling and let it dominate your day.

I R-E-A-C-H to Forgive

Forgiveness is often challenging. In those instances the five-step acronym REACH can nudge us along.

R – stands for recalling the hurt as objectively as possible.
E – stands for empathy; here it means to be able to contextualize and understand the point of view of the person who has wronged you.
A – is for your altruistic gift of forgiveness; we can all recall a time when we unknowingly hurt someone and were forgiven.
C – stands for the committing to publically forgive, not just privately in your heart.
H – stands for holding onto forgiveness and not being swayed by the mixed feelings that will inevitably arise.

The REACH method of forgiveness comes from the work of Everett Worthington, a psychologist who studies forgiveness.

Gratitude is the Fix for a Grumpy Heart

There is so much evidence now for the life-enhancing effects of practicing gratitude. Not only has it been shown to improve clinical depression, but it is thought to create and increase happiness.

If you have a grumpy heart, simply acknowledge this (without judgment). You may have noticed that people avoid you even though you actually like them and desire their company. The alienation is what makes you feel sad, angry and lonely. The fix for your grumpy heart is to regularly practice expressing gratitude. The practice of giving gratitude can prevent your grumpiness from solidifying, and keeps the terrain of relationship soft enough so that you remain receptive to the love of others. This can then allow you to feel warm and optimistic, thereby transforming your heart.

Soothe Your Heart with a Breath Meditation

You must breathe in order to live. In other words, breath is life. This is why the breath is considered divine.

Modern life makes many demands on us and we often do not breathe properly and freely. Mostly we are unaware of how we breathe and even of the fact that we breathe. It is not until we go on holiday that we can relax, and really experience our breath, and appreciate the sensation of the air and of the earth. Sometimes when we are away from our familiar surroundings we can notice that the air smells different and we recognize that we are breathing in a more relaxed fashion. When we are sufficiently relaxed, our heartbeat and breathing are able to harmonize and this promotes a state of well-being.

There is a good chance that your breathing pattern has been disrupted if you are scattered, or if you are experiencing sadness or anxiety, or if your energy is generally poor. It might highlight that you've been breathing sub-optimally all along. The regular practice of simple abdominal breathing will help tremendously. Over time, you will note that your sleep improves as well.

Abdominal breathing is an ideal way to relax or to soothe yourself. It's good to practice at fixed times during the day or informally whenever you feel you need to settle or anchor yourself. It's also an excellent way for melting away sadness and grief.

Sit or lie down comfortably. Place one hand on your abdomen over the navel. Breathe out slowly and completely. Notice that your navel moves towards the spine. Hold your breath for a second. Breathe in slowly and deeply. Notice that your navel rises. Hold your breath for a second or so. Repeat for 10-20 cycles.

Notice how you were able to tune in to your body and slow down your breathing rate. Note that you feel calm and mentally clear. Train yourself to take that feeling of calm forward with you.

Heart-to-Heart Talk with My Inner Advisor

Each of us has an Inner Advisor deep within. Learn to let your Inner Advisor grow within you so that you may consult with this dimension of yourself, wherever you are, at any time. The answer to a problem or a dilemma often resides within you or in this "other-in" dimension. We must simply learn to slow down and access this part, and have the conversation. Repeatedly do this visualization so that you can achieve a level of comfort and use this technique whenever the need arises. As you get better at it, you will see that it is possible to have a heart-to-heart "conversation" with your Inner Advisor. You will build trust and self-confidence within yourself.

Sit comfortably in your favorite chair. Breathe comfortably and deeply. Close your eyes and look out as if you are looking onto your room, life-size or even larger. See that there is another chair, just like the one you are sitting in, across from you. Let yourself see the form of a person there, not yourself or someone you know, but just a form.

Train yourself to trust this all-accepting, non-judgmental presence. Silently pose a question. You may speak directly from your heart. You can bring up anything you wish. Listen for the response. Train yourself to listen for the response. It may not be what you are expecting. Try not to have an expectation of the answer.

Allow yourself to fully consider the response. If there is some information you would like to leave with your Inner Advisor so that it can be mulled over, you can do so; you can continue at another time. Then, when you feel ready, say goodbye, take a deep breath, and return to the here and now. Allow yourself to feel lightness of heart.

Train yourself to experience this feeling after you have unburdened yourself in the heart-to-heart conversation with your Inner Advisor. Take the light-heartedness forward with you for the remainder of your day. Treat it as a wonderful and precious feeling and let it dominate your day.

Sitting Gratitude Meditation

Sometimes we think we run out of things for which to be grateful. Just think of one thing and try this meditation. It can be done in the morning or evening. You can stay with the same item for a week if you like, and see what evolves.

Sit in the meditation position. Be comfortable and breathe mindfully. Close your eyes or keep a soft gaze. Consider one thing for which you can sincerely be thankful. It could even be the beauty of nature. Continue for at least ten minutes. Notice the thoughts, feelings, and bodily sensations you experience. Whatever you are doing is right; there is no wrong way to do this. When you feel ready, allow yourself to come back to the here and now.

How I Increase Happiness

Happiness can take the form of straightforward joy. It can also take the form of satisfaction, flow, Samadhi, savoring, vital engagement, meaning and purpose, or contentment or gratitude, or santosa.

Aside from different definitions of happiness across the world, the quality of the feeling of happiness differs as well. In some cultures there is more energy associated with what is considered to be a happy state, whereas other cultures view quieter aspects like peace, tranquility and harmony as integral to happiness.

It's helpful to think of happiness as an experience or process, as opposed to a destination.

Another helpful tip when considering your happiness is to shift the emphasis to what you "put" into your heart, rather than what you are trying to remove. Sow seeds of "happy" experiences in order to reap "happy" experiences. If you want to be happy, focus on being happy.

Here's the meditation I do when I need or want to increase my sense of happiness: I

visualize an image of an experience that has
made me feel peaceful, intact, and full of
joy. My favorite image is an exquisite,
early-morning landscape from a trip in
Tuscany. I mentally bring that image before
me. I can see the early morning fog and
behind that, the mountainous landscape of
Montalcino. The backdrop is a beautiful,
azure sky. The land rolls out and I can see
fields. I can see the flowers closer to me. I
can even smell the lavender. The morning
air is fresh and crisp and I can feel the
coolness on my skin. I'm holding a cup of
freshly made cappuccino. I can feel the
warmth of the mug with my hands and I
love the aroma of the coffee. The taste is
rich and robust. I hear the cicadas singing,
and I feel great and in harmony with nature.

I recall as much detail as possible, creating a
full sensory experience. I recognize how
absolutely wonderful I feel. I breathe in this
happiness through my heart-center. I focus
on this sense of happiness and mentally let it
grow within until I am filled with happiness.
I direct myself to hold onto that happy
feeling as something precious and I carry it
forward.

In my outer life I recognize I cannot govern
what may come my way. But I do have

control over what is in my heart. I have the ability to select what will or will not enter my heart. My heart is the reservoir of my past, present, and future and that of the entire universe. The human heart doesn't seem to care about the passage of linear time. All is present at any given moment, and this is the fullness of the moment. All is held tightly, and loosely, in a single moment.

Tina Chadda, MD

Heart

So much of what we are, we owe to our heart. It keeps us alive through pumping blood and nutrients through our body, but keeps us emotionally connected and present through the deep sentiment and passion that resonates within it. A full heart is a happy one, and will beat strong, and will warm those around you. Care for your heart. Guard your heart, and always be sensitive and aware of its needs.

If you find your heart is injured or damaged, take the time to allow it to rebuild and repair. Remember, your heart is as strong as the person caring for it. But most importantly, we are only given one heart. It will stay with us through thick and thin, the good and the bad, the happy and the sad. As you grow, so will your heart. As you age, your heart will age beside you. Allow your heart all that it deserves so it can give you all that you deserve. Your heart is a true companion and gift that you should celebrate each and every day.

- 156 -

Parting Words: Secrets of the Heart

"The men where you live," said the little prince, "raise five thousand roses in the same garden — and they do not find in it what they are looking for."

"They do not find it," I replied.

"And yet what they are looking for could be found in one single rose, or a little water."

"Yes, that is true," I said.

And the little prince added: "But the eyes are blind. One must look with the heart..."

Antoine de Saint-Exupéry

I love this passage from the timeless tale, *The Little Prince*. I discovered it in childhood and I return to it every once in awhile, always finding it instructive and comforting. The words seem to cover the secret contained in the human heart, an essential lesson on being human. Share this passage with your loved ones, and your children.

What is it that we are looking for? Love, as symbolized by the rose, or survival, represented by "a little water." Interestingly enough, Saint-Exupéry positions the rose before the water. It's also possible that Saint-Exupéry equates love with water, indicating that he believed both are necessary for life.

And how do we look? We "look with the heart," wrote Saint-Exupéry.

It is in the repository of the human heart where we experience the confluence of sorrow, joy, and desire. Everything comes together within that complicated and beautiful muscle. This rich and sometimes volatile concoction is like a magical primordial soup. Its functions range from simple lubrication, to feeling, to healing. The heart is the matrix for our emotional life. This explains the metonymical phrase of, "Have a heart."

Desire is your life force, your longing or passion. Never let it evaporate because it's essential to being human, as Saint-Exupéry seems to convey to us in the quote above. It's what keeps us searching while binding us to suffering at the same time. Without desire in the heart, we become apathetic, and unable to blossom. To walk the path of desire is to engage with life rather than to tread its surface.

Desire is a complex emotion and it can be a confusing word because it's closely related to love. Love, of course, is such a grand word. But it is precisely because of its grandness, with all of its subtlety and complexity, that we continue the search. The twists and turns in the search represent our upsets. These frustrations are inevitable, and are simply perversions of love and must not deter us on our journey.

Rapture, rupture, and repair are simultaneously present in the heart. Perhaps what's most amazing about the human heart is that it can be a self-balancing system when even the slightest care is given. Life's challenges can be transformed into resilience and strength as you heal your heart.

As Saint-Exupéry indicates, a single rose will suffice. The subject and object are one in the same. That's because a single rose, delicate yet strong, has the stand-alone power to represent an entire universe. A rose simply is; it does not have to be anything more than it already is. A rose is perfect as it is and requires no embellishment. What's more, is that a rosebud, like the heart, is genetically programmed to blossom into a beautiful form. It seems to not matter the color of the rose, as each hue represents a different facet of love. Through that powerful force of love, we discover the richness of being human.

Love is the strongest, most positive and potent force in the universe. Love is, and creates, a vortex of attraction from which all goodness and achievement derive.

For my readers- tend to your heart. It is the core, the essence, of you and you literally cannot exist without it. Nurture and heal you heart. Let it open and blossom like a rose. Let love be your state of well-being and the wellspring of your life.

My wish is that this book, and the meditations and reflections in it, motivate and inspire your heart to beat with greater purpose and excessive warmth. Through taking the time to consider just a few of these powerful and meaningful principles during each waking day, you will push your heart to welcome in a greater level of happiness. That happiness will then be projected to the world and be a conduit for more happiness, much like a heart is the conduit for the movement of essential nutrients and blood to all parts of the body.

You are your own heart, destined to connect and be the medium that manifests change and a better tomorrow. Be the heart you hope to see in the world. And through that simple mission, we can all love more and reach unparalleled levels of joy.

Epilogue: Beggarly Heart

When the heart is hard and parched up,
come upon me with a shower of mercy.

When grace is lost from life,
come with a burst of song.

When tumultuous work raises its din on all
sides shutting me
out from
beyond, come to me, my lord of silence,
with thy peace and
rest.

When my beggarly heart sits crouched, shut
up in a corner,
break open the door, my king, and come
with the ceremony of
a king.

When desire blinds the mind with delusion
and dust, O thou
holy one,
thou wakeful, come with thy light and thy
thunder.
-Rabindranath Tagor